W9-CKM-736

THE STORY OF THE
SAN DIEGO CHARGERS

NFL TODAY

THE STORY OF THE SAN DIEGO CHARGERS

TYLER OMOTH

CREATIVE EDUCATION

Cover: Quarterback John Hadl (top), quarterback
Philip Rivers (bottom)
Page 2: Wide receiver Vincent Jackson
Pages 4–5: Tight end Antonio Gates (left) and
quarterback Philip Rivers (right)
Pages 6–7: Defensive end Igor Olshansky

....

Published by Creative Education
P.O. Box 227, Mankato, Minnesota 56002
Creative Education is an imprint of
The Creative Company
www.thecreativecompany.us

Design and production by Blue Design
Design Associate: Sarah Yakawonis
Printed in the United States of America

Photographs by AP Images, Getty Images (K.C.
Alfred/Union-Tribune, Dave Cross/NFL, David
Drapkin, Stephen Dunn, Stephen Dunn/Allsport,
Paul Jasienski, Gene Lower/NFL, Donald Miralle,
Ronald C. Modra/Sports Imagery, NFL Photos, Al
Messerschmidt, Donald Miralle, Darryl Norenberg/
NFL, Doug Pensinger, George Rose, Paul Spinelli, Rick
Stewart, Greg Trott, Charles Aqua Viva/NFL, Todd
Warshaw, Stuart Westmorland, Marilynn Young/AFP)

Library of Congress Cataloging-in-Publication Data

Omoth, Tyler.
The story of the San Diego Chargers / by Tyler
Omoth.
p. cm. — (NFL today)
Includes index.
ISBN 978-1-58341-769-0
1. San Diego Chargers (Football team)—History—
Juvenile literature. I. Title. II. Series.

GV956.S29066 2009
796.332'6409794985—dc22   2008022700

First Edition
9 8 7 6 5 4 3 2 1

CONTENTS

ON THE SIDELINES

MEET THE CHARGERS

CHARGING FROM THE GATE

Located just north of Mexico on the coast of the Pacific Ocean, San Diego is the second-largest city in California. Founded by Spanish missionaries in 1769, San Diego was seized by Mexico in 1822. It later came under the control of the United States during the Mexican-American War, officially becoming a U.S. city in 1850. Today, this beautiful port city is home to more than one million people—and one National Football League (NFL) team: the San Diego Chargers.

The team was originally formed in Los Angeles in 1959 as a member of the new American Football League (AFL). The team's original owner was Barron Hilton, the son of hotel mogul Conrad Hilton. Through a public "name-the-team" contest, the name "Chargers" was suggested. Hilton and general manager Frank Ready liked the fighting spirit of the name, and the Los Angeles Chargers were soon outfitted in sharp-looking uniforms of blue and gold, complete with lightning bolts on the helmets and pants.

As befitted a team with a lightning bolt for a logo, the Chargers electrified their fans from the start. The team's first coach, Sid Gillman, had previously won an NFL championship while coaching the Los Angeles Rams, and he set out to lead the Chargers to championship glory as well. With a talented roster featuring running back Paul Lowe and quarterback

X Besides its sports history and spectacular weather, the port city of San Diego is known for its long beaches, large Latino population, and numerous regional military facilities.

Jack Kemp, the Chargers went 10–4 in 1960 and won the AFL's

Western Division. Although they lost to the Houston Oilers

in the AFL Championship Game, the good times were just

beginning. Those good times would not be in Los Angeles,

though. L.A. fans were less than enthusiastic about the new

team. So, in 1961, the Chargers moved down the California

coast to San Diego.

In San Diego, the team surrounded Lowe and Kemp with

more talent by drafting running back Keith Lincoln and

defensive linemen Earl Faison and Ernie Ladd. These players

carried the Chargers to another Western Division title in 1961.

Unfortunately, the Oilers again topped the Chargers for the

AFL championship.

Looking for a boost that would finally push them to

the top, the Chargers traded for a quick and sure-handed

receiver named Lance Alworth in 1962. In 1963, Alworth—

nicknamed "Bambi" because of his deer-like grace and

energy—gave the team that boost by posting 1,205 receiving

yards and scoring 11 touchdowns. With Alworth and two new

quarterbacks, veteran Tobin Rote and youngster John Hadl,

sparking the AFL's most explosive passing attack, San Diego

crushed the Denver Broncos in the last game of the season to

win its division yet again.

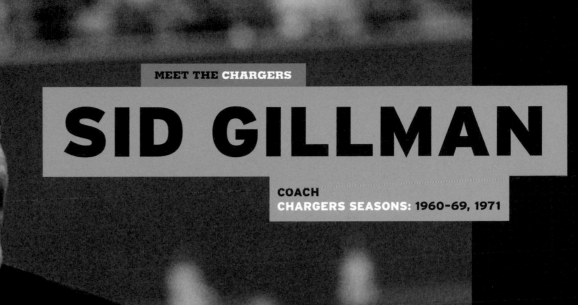

SID GILLMAN

COACH
CHARGERS SEASONS: 1960–69, 1971

In the very first College versus Pros All-Star Game in 1934, a young end named Sid Gillman had a revelution. After Chicago Bears fullback Bronko Nagurski laid a punishing hit on him, he realized that he could have a longer and healthier career as a coach than he could as a player. In an era when the running game was the bread and butter of any offense, Gillman was convinced of the big-play possibilities of a high-powered passing attack. By implementing his high-scoring passing strategies, he led the Chargers to five divisional crowns in the AFL's first six seasons and won the AFL championship in 1963. The league was forced to adapt to his style of play just to compete with the Chargers. "The Chargers' image of the lightning bolt was perfect for Sid Gillman and how his teams played football," said Alex Spanos, who took ownership of the Chargers in the 1980s. Gillman was innovative in his use of game film as a method of preparing his team for its next matchup. He was also the first head coach to win divisional titles in both the AFL and the NFL.

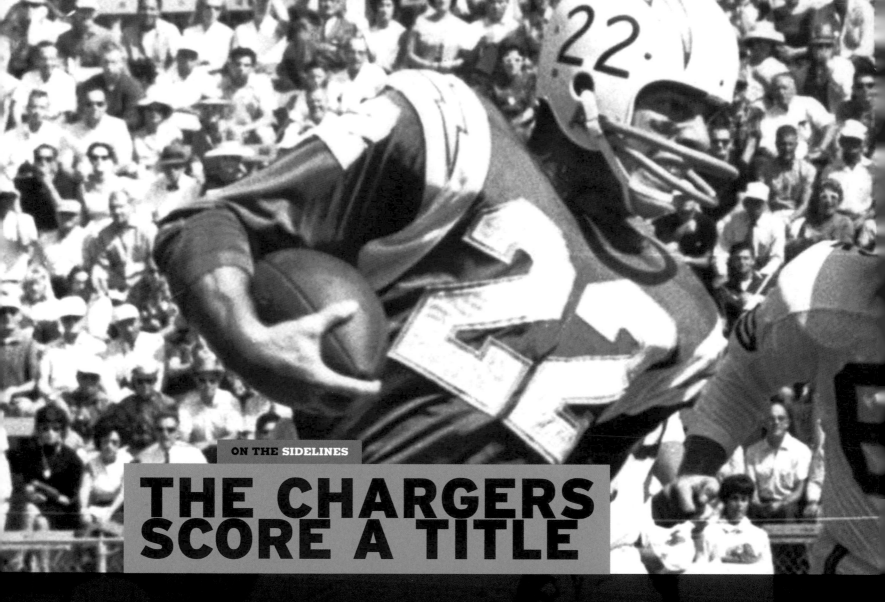

THE CHARGERS SCORE A TITLE

After the 1963 season, a tie in the AFL's Eastern Division prompted a special playoff matchup between the Boston Patriots and the Buffalo Bills. Boston won the game easily and traveled to Balboa Stadium in San Diego to take on the Chargers in the AFL Championship Game. The Chargers had been in the big game twice before—as the Los Angeles Chargers in the very first AFL title game and again in 1961 after moving to San Diego—but had come up short both times. The "Bolts" started the scoring in the 1963 title game with a touchdown run by quarterback Tobin Rote. Boston had made its way to the championship game with a much-heralded defense, but the Chargers quickly proved that they could score at will. Running back Keith Lincoln (pictured) led the way with 349 yards in total offense and 2 touchdowns. By game's end, the Chargers had drubbed the Patriots 51–10 for their first championship. Although they would approach championship heights after that, as of 2008, that 1963 triumph remained the Chargers' only league title.

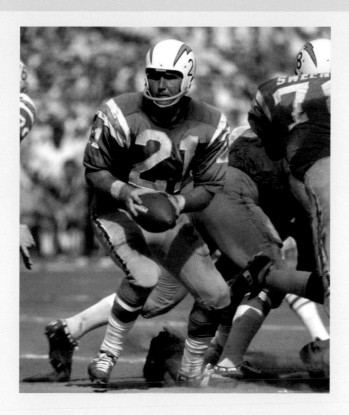

San Diego fans rejoiced as the Chargers then finally won their first AFL championship, demolishing the Boston Patriots 51–10. In that game, the Chargers' offense was nearly unstoppable, and Lincoln blasted through the Patriots' defense for 206 rushing yards. "This isn't a football team," said Boston's awestruck coach, Mike Hovak. "It's a machine."

The Chargers machine continued to run at full throttle in 1964 and 1965. San Diego returned to the AFL Championship Game both years, only to lose to the Buffalo Bills both times. Alworth and Hadl continued their offensive heroics, but the departure of Ladd in 1965 and Faison in 1966 hurt the team. Over the next three seasons, San Diego put together mediocre records. The Chargers had lost their championship luster.

In 1970, the AFL and NFL merged, beginning a new era in professional football. In their 10 AFL seasons, the Chargers had won 5 division titles and 1 league championship. But the team had grown old. In 1970, even the greats failed to put up great numbers, as Alworth's production dropped off and Hadl completed fewer than half of his passes. After the 1971 season, Gillman stepped down as head coach.

General manager Harland Svare took over as coach after Gillman's departure, and the team began to completely rebuild its roster. Within a year, Svare had pulled the trigger on 21 trades. In 1973, the Chargers brought in veteran quarterback Johnny Unitas to replace the traded Hadl, but Unitas was no better. Rookie quarterback Dan Fouts took over, but he threw a high volume of interceptions, and the 1973 Chargers finished a woeful 2–11–1.

In 1974, Tommy Prothro took over as the Chargers' new head coach, and the team took the field with a new look, having traded its old, white helmets for blue ones. Despite these changes, the team's play on the field remained consistently poor. Fouts continued to struggle with interceptions for the next few years, and San Diego strung together losing seasons through 1976. Yet the team continued to believe in Fouts—and that trust would soon pay off.

LANCE ALWORTH

WIDE RECEIVER
CHARGERS SEASONS: 1962-70
HEIGHT: 6 FEET
WEIGHT: 184 POUNDS

Some football players succeed with hard work and determination. Others, such as Lance Alworth, seem to be born stars, possessing rare natural speed and grace. Recognizing that the San Diego Chargers needed a deep threat on offense in the early 1960s, assistant coach Al Davis tenaciously pushed for the Chargers to acquire the services of Alworth, who was drafted by the AFL's Oakland Raiders in 1962. Chargers management listened and soon swung a trade to bring Alworth to San Diego. In the early years of the AFL, the Chargers were a team that embraced a fast-paced, crowd-pleasing brand of football, and Alworth was at the center of that excitement. The receiver known as "Bambi" was a constant big-play threat. In 9 years with the Chargers, he averaged more than 1,000 yards per season. "Lance Alworth was one of maybe three players in my lifetime who had what I would call 'it'," said Davis. "You could see right from the beginning that he was going to be a superstar." In 1978, Alworth became the very first AFL player to be enshrined in the Pro Football Hall of Fame.

FLYING WITH AIR CORYELL

x - - - - - - - - - - - - - - - - - -

X A ball boy for the San Francisco 49ers as a youngster, Dan Fouts forged a Hall of Fame career farther down the California coast, leading the Chargers in the 1970s and '80s.

Finally, in 1978, the Chargers achieved their first winning season (9–7) of the decade. Even then, though, the team took its share of lumps. Early in that season, San Diego fans saw their team fall victim to one of the most infamous plays in franchise history, known as the Oakland Raiders' "Holy Roller" play. Trailing the Chargers 14–20 with just 10 seconds left in the fourth quarter, the Raiders intentionally and repeatedly fumbled the ball forward until they could fall on it in the end zone to win the game. The play infuriated Chargers fans and players and led to an NFL rule change limiting the offense's ability to advance a fumble on fourth downs or in the final two minutes of a game. Thanks in part to that defeat, San Diego started the season 1–4 before Don Coryell stepped in as the club's new head coach in midseason. Coach Coryell seemed to bring the necessary winning touch, as the Chargers surged to seven victories in their final eight games.

Coach Coryell deserved much of the credit for the Chargers' sudden success, but so did Fouts. In 1979, the seventh-year quarterback finally emerged as a genuine star, setting a new NFL single-season record by passing for 4,082 yards. His precise passing helped propel the Chargers to a 12–4 record and an American Football Conference (AFC) West Division championship—their first division title since 1965. With Fouts leading Coryell's brilliant, pass-oriented offense, sportswriters began calling the Chargers' passing attack "Air Coryell."

Behind Don and Dan, San Diego began to look like the Chargers of old. From 1979 to 1981, the team won the AFC West

Although knee injuries ended his career by age 30, tight end Kellen Winslow was dynamite when healthy, catching more passes than any other NFL player in 1980 and 1981. **X**

X Wideout Wes Chandler used his speed to stretch defenses and catch long bombs as part of San Diego's "Air Coryell" offense.

ON THE SIDELINES

A SINGULAR ALL-STAR GAME

During the 1965 season, the AFL toyed with a new postseason All-Star Game format, pitting an AFL All-Star squad against the league's championship team from that year. That year it was the Buffalo Bills who had won it all and were slated to match up against an All-Star team consisting of the AFL's very best, including several Chargers stars. San Diego quarterback John Hadl (pictured, right) started the game, and running back Paul Lowe capped a third-quarter drive with a one-yard touchdown plunge. The Chargers' star receiver, Lance Alworth (pictured, left), was not supposed to play in the game due to a rib injury, but he came up big with two touchdown catches, getting knocked unconscious during the second catch and carried from the field at Houston's Rice Stadium to a standing ovation. Chargers linebacker Frank Buncom also helped the All-Stars attain a 30–19 victory over the Bills, winning Defensive Player of the Game honors. The All-Stars proved to be more than the Bills could handle, and in 1967, the AFL returned to its old Eastern Division versus Western Division All-Star Game format.

title every year and posted a combined 33–15 record. And every year, Fouts just seemed to get better. In 1981, the quarterback that many considered the toughest in the NFL broke his own single-season passing record for the third straight year, throwing for a whopping 4,802 yards and 33 touchdowns.

Unfortunately, the biggest prize of all eluded the Chargers, who could never quite reach the Super Bowl. In 1981, the team lost in the AFC Championship Game for the second straight season, despite having a loaded roster that included Pro Bowl defensive linemen Gary "Big Hands" Johnson, Louie Kelcher, and Fred Dean. "I can't tell you how much it hurts to come this far and lose two years in a row," Coach Coryell said sadly after the 1981 title game loss to the Cincinnati Bengals.

The Chargers made the playoffs again in 1982, only to fall to the Miami Dolphins in the second round. The team's defense was dealt a terrible blow after the season when Johnson, Kelcher, and Dean all left town. Then, as they had a decade earlier, the Chargers slipped into a losing slump that would last most of the decade.

As injuries began to slow down Fouts, receiver Charlie Joiner remained one of the few consistent bright spots for San Diego during those years. At 5-foot-11 and 185 pounds, Joiner was rather small by NFL standards, but he made up for it with a powerful mixture of instincts and toughness. Joiner quietly posted four 1,000-yard seasons over the course of an amazing 18-season NFL career. Before he finally retired after the 1986 season at the age of 39, he would catch 750 passes for 12,146 yards—both NFL records.

Although the Chargers of the '80s featured other outstanding passing targets—including star tight end Kellen Winslow and receivers John Jefferson and Wes Chandler—the one constant link was Joiner. "I don't recall him ever missing a practice at all since I've been in San Diego," Coach Coryell said. "One time, he cracked a rib and didn't take a day off. He said, 'I'll work through it.'"

Except for the efforts of Joiner and his fellow receivers, the mid-1980s were some dark seasons for San Diego. In 1986, the team found a new defensive star as rookie end Leslie O'Neal made 12.5 quarterback sacks to win the NFL Defensive Rookie of the Year award; he would go on to a career that featured six Pro Bowl appearances. The Chargers started 8–1 a year later but stumbled down the stretch and missed the playoffs again. Fouts and Winslow retired after that, leaving San Diego fans to hope for better things in the 1990s.

DAN FOUTS

QUARTERBACK
CHARGERS SEASONS: 1973-87
HEIGHT: 6-FOOT-3
WEIGHT: 204 POUNDS

A football team that loves to throw the deep ball needs a quarterback with a big arm, intelligence, and the toughness to take a hit. The San Diego Chargers found all of those attributes in Dan Fouts. While he lacked great running speed, Fouts excelled at standing in the pocket and reading the field. And when he found his target, he would deliver a tight spiral with his powerful right arm. The Chargers' high-powered offense of the late 1970s and early '80s was called "Air Coryell" after the coach who designed the passing plays, but Fouts was the engine that made it work. The Chargers went from a mediocre football team to a perennial contender, winning the AFC West in 1979, 1980, and 1981. The longtime Chargers quarterback was a six-time Pro-Bowler, a three-time All-Pro, and winner of the NFL Most Valuable Player (MVP) award in 1982. Ernie Zambese, the team's offensive coordinator during the Air Coryell era, knew he had something special in his quarterback, saying, "Dan Fouts had a tremendous ability to focus, unlike anyone else I've ever seen, and he was an unbelievable leader."

BEATHARD'S
BOLTS

After finishing dead last in the AFC West in 1989, San Diego hired a new general manager it believed could ignite the "Bolts" once again: Bobby Beathard. Widely considered one of the smartest men in the NFL, Beathard had been responsible a decade earlier for rebuilding the Washington Redskins. Chargers management hoped he would work similar magic in San Diego.

Beathard quickly proved his genius by selecting linebacker Junior Seau out of the University of Southern California with San Diego's top pick in the 1990 NFL Draft. An incredibly powerful player who could bench-press 500 pounds, Seau became an instant terror in the NFL as the heart of San Diego's defense. Bill Belichick, the head coach of the Cleveland Browns, was astounded by the Chargers' new star. "Junior Seau is the best defensive player we've faced, I'd say, by a pretty good margin," said Belichick.

After San Diego posted losing records in 1990 and 1991, Beathard continued to rebuild. In 1992, he hired a new head coach: Bobby Ross, who had just led Georgia Tech University

Linebacker Junior Seau was both a one-man wrecking crew and a model of consistency, leading all Chargers defenders in tackles every season of his San Diego career. **X**

THE EPIC IN MIAMI

Some football games are played so well by both teams that it seems wrong that either team should lose. The 1982 playoff game between the Chargers and the Miami Dolphins was one such game, an epic battle that is remembered as one of the best in NFL history. After the Chargers jumped out to a 24–0 lead in the first quarter, the Dolphins inserted backup quarterback Don Strock and used a trick "hook and lateral" play to score at the end of the half, bringing the score to 24–17. The second half found the two teams in a 38–38 tie as the Dolphins lined up for a last-second, 43-yard field goal to win the game. But San Diego tight end Kellen Winslow, who was battling injuries and dehydration, blocked the Dolphins' field-goal attempt. In overtime, kicker Rolf Benirschke finally hit a 29-yard field goal to give the Chargers the victory. The exhausting "Epic in Miami" set a number of NFL playoffs records, including most combined points (79), most combined yards (1,036), and most combined passing yards (836).

to the 1990 national college championship. Beathard then picked up a new quarterback by signing former Washington Redskins signal-caller Stan Humphries. With these new pieces in place, the 1992 Chargers made a startling comeback, winning their first AFC West title in more than a decade with an 11–5 record.

The team slipped to 8–8 in 1993, as Humphries missed most of the season with an injury. When the Chargers took the field in 1994, it was with a healthy roster and a new weapon in rookie running back Natrone Means. After finishing the season 11–5 and receiving a first-round bye in the postseason, San Diego set its sights on nothing less than a Super Bowl victory.

The joyride continued in San Diego as the Chargers beat the Dolphins and a heavily favored Pittsburgh Steelers team in two thrilling playoff games to win the AFC championship and then headed to Miami for their first Super Bowl. "We were very much underdogs," Humphries later said of San Diego's playoff run. "Pittsburgh was doing their Super Bowl videos already, getting ready for that. You kind of go into the game and just let it all go and know you've got nothing to lose." Seau, Means, and the rest of the Chargers would fall one

CHARLIE JOINER

WIDE RECEIVER
CHARGERS SEASONS: 1976-86
HEIGHT: 5-FOOT-11
WEIGHT: 188 POUNDS

Charlie Joiner was drafted as a defensive back in 1969 by the Houston Oilers, but after playing briefly on defense and special teams, Joiner switched to offense as a wide receiver. When Joiner was traded to the Chargers in 1976, he realized his true potential and became a star. He was a crucial part of the Chargers' run to the AFC Championship Game in 1981 and 1982. Joiner combined his physical gifts with precise route running and a head for the game that made him a consistent playmaker. He was a smart and unassuming player who preferred to make his mark on the field rather than by talking. As quarterback Dan Fouts piloted the Chargers' offense, Joiner was usually his first, and best, target. San Francisco 49ers coaching legend Bill Walsh once called Joiner "the most intelligent, the smartest, the most calculating receiver the game has ever known." In January 2008, the Chargers hired Joiner as their wide receivers coach, hoping he would pass some of his wisdom along to the team's receiving corps.

win short of an NFL championship, though, losing to the San Francisco 49ers by a score of 49–26.

The Chargers returned to the playoffs in 1995, but the year ended in disappointment with a 35–20 loss to the Indianapolis Colts. The Chargers had once again peaked without winning it all. Seau and such players as receiver Tony Martin continued to shine, but it wasn't enough. The Bolts went 8–8 in 1996, then crashed to the AFC West cellar again, finishing the 1997 season 4–12.

Determined to build the team back up with youth, Beathard and the Chargers traded two veteran players and

Although his team came up short on the scoreboard, halfback Ronnie Harmon gave a great effort versus the 49ers in Super Bowl XXIX, catching eight passes. **X**

what amounted to two seasons' worth of draft choices to the Arizona Cardinals for the right to the second overall pick in the 1998 NFL Draft. With it, San Diego selected Ryan Leaf, a promising, 6-foot-5 quarterback out of Washington State University. Hoping that Leaf would lead the team forward after adjusting to the pro game, the Chargers and their fans waited … and waited. Leaf never emerged as the star the team needed, and the Chargers continued to fade. After an embarrassing 2000 season in which the team went 1–15 and Leaf alienated teammates and the media with temper tantrums and immature behavior, San Diego released the quarterback.

After going through three coaches in four rocky seasons, San Diego hired veteran NFL coach Marty Schottenheimer to take charge of the team in 2002. Although the Chargers had gone just 5–11 the year before, Schottenheimer inherited a team with potential. In the 2001 NFL Draft, the Chargers had used the fifth overall pick to grab LaDainian Tomlinson, a shifty and highly touted running back out of Texas Christian University. They had also drafted a tough young quarterback named Drew Brees.

Behind Coach Schottenheimer's leadership and the great play of Tomlinson—who rushed for 1,683 yards—the 2002

JUNIOR SEAU

LINEBACKER
CHARGERS SEASONS: 1990-2002
HEIGHT: 6-FOOT-3
WEIGHT: 248 POUNDS

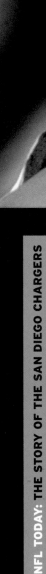

Like the lightning bolt on his helmet, Junior Seau moved fast and struck hard. Nicknamed "The Tasmanian Devil," Seau played with remarkable energy and a nose for the ball. He was a superb all-around defender who was able to rush the quarterback, chase down ballcarriers from sideline to sideline, and even drop back into pass coverage. While Chargers fans adored their hard-hitting linebacker for his relentless hustle and flair for the game, the fist-pumping "lightning bolt dance" Seau sometimes showcased to celebrate big plays didn't always go over so well with opponents. He soon abandoned his notorious dance but continued to wreak havoc on opposing offenses, becoming one of only four players since the 1970 NFL-AFL merger to appear in 12 straight Pro Bowls. In San Diego's Super Bowl appearance after the 1994 season, he tallied 11 tackles and 1 sack. His energy and leadership on the field affected the whole team. "He brought something to the game that very few people have brought to the game," former Chargers general manager Bobby Beathard said. "He made people around him better."

Chargers proved that they were no longer pushovers. By the end of the season, the team was 8–8 and had given its fans reasons for optimism. Although the San Diego faithful were saddened when 12-time Pro-Bowler Junior Seau left town after the season, they were encouraged by Tomlinson's emergence as one of the NFL's most dangerous ballcarriers. "I've never coached a running back that has the kind of explosive change of direction he's got," Schottenheimer said of the young star. "He's got the ability to see things and make cuts that a lot of the winning running backs in this league don't have." The veteran coach and the new running back would need a little time, but they would soon have the Chargers flying high.

The 13th head coach in Chargers history, Marty Schottenheimer had the good fortune of having sensational halfback LaDainian Tomlinson (left) on the roster when he arrived in 2002. **X**

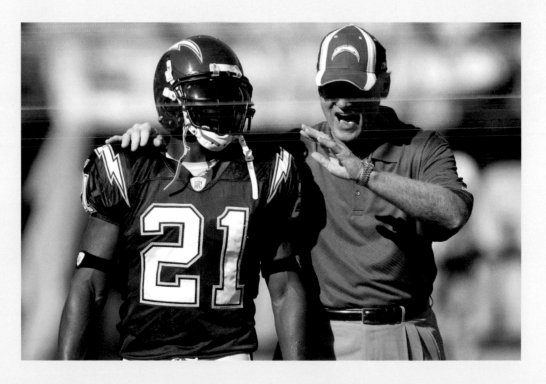

A CONTENDER
AGAIN

X-----

The Bolts dropped their first five games in 2003. Then, after ending their losing streak against the Cleveland Browns, disaster hit the San Diego area in the form of two wildfires that forced the team to play a Monday Night Football "home" game in Sun Devil Stadium in Tempe, Arizona. Despite the efforts of popular, 41-year-old backup quarterback Doug Flutie, the Chargers continued to struggle, finishing the season a dismal 4–12.

The silver lining to the dark cloud of the 2003 season was that the Chargers' record earned them the number-one pick in the 2004 NFL Draft. However, the team's bad luck continued as their top choice, quarterback Eli Manning, declared that he would not play for the Chargers, forcing them to trade him to the New York Giants for the fourth overall pick—quarterback Philip Rivers—plus future draft picks.

After scoring just 38 touchdowns in all of 2003, the Chargers came alive in a big way in 2004, finding the end zone 55 times. Brees had an exceptional year with 27 touchdown passes, and Tomlinson continued to cement his standing as arguably the game's best running back with 18 touchdowns. Additionally, a new offensive weapon emerged in the form of tight end Antonio Gates. Although Gates had been largely dedicated to basketball throughout his college career, he

X Big, agile, and with a knack for getting open, Antonio Gates emerged as a star in 2004, earning All-Pro honors as the NFL's best tight end for the first of three straight seasons.

signed with the Chargers as an undrafted free agent and put his size and natural athleticism to use, becoming a big-play threat. Coach Schottenheimer admitted that the Chargers struck gold through dumb luck with the tight end. "If we had known he was going to be that good, we would have picked him number one instead of signing him as a free agent," he said.

San Diego used its new offensive firepower to win the AFC West title for the first time since 1994. However, the celebration was short-lived, as the New York Jets came into San Diego's Qualcomm Stadium in the playoffs and took care of the Chargers in overtime by a score of 20–17.

X At 6-foot-5, wideout Vincent Jackson provided a big passing target for quarterbacks Drew Brees and Philip Rivers.

SUPER SOUTHERN CALIFORNIA

It was an all-California matchup as the underdog Chargers faced the powerhouse San Francisco 49ers at Miami's Joe Robbie Stadium to cap off the 1994 season in Super Bowl XXIX. The 49ers took an early 14–0 lead, but running back Natrone Means's one-yard touchdown run put the Chargers on the board. The Bolts would eventually get touchdowns on a 98-yard Andre Coleman kickoff return and a Tony Martin reception, but the high-powered aerial attack of the 49ers was more than San Diego's defense could handle. San Francisco went on to win the game 49–26 as both teams set records. It was the first Super Bowl to have both teams score in every quarter. After Coleman's kick return for a touchdown, quarterback Stan Humphries completed a pass to receiver Mark Seay for the first two-point conversion in Super Bowl history. Humphries later hit tight end Alfred Papunu for a second two-point conversion, but the 49ers offense was simply too much. Although the Chargers came up short in their first Super Bowl appearance, they left their mark on Super Bowl history.

LaDAINIAN TOMLINSON

RUNNING BACK
CHARGERS SEASONS: 2001–PRESENT
HEIGHT: 5-FOOT-10
WEIGHT: 221 POUNDS

He had the speed. He had the toughness. He could run like an elite back, catch passes like a top-flight receiver, and, when needed, could be a tenacious blocker. In short, when the San Diego Chargers drafted LaDainian Tomlinson in 2001, they got one of the most complete backs the game has ever seen. Between 2001 and 2007, "L. T." never had fewer than 1,200 rushing yards and 300 receiving yards in any season with the Chargers. Yards make for great stats, but points win games, and Tomlinson had a nose for the end zone like few other players. In 2006, he broke the NFL single-season touchdown record by crossing the goal line an amazing 31 times. Even other star NFL rushers were impressed. "I'm happy for him," said Arizona Cardinals running back Edgerrin James. "He deserves it. He's been ballin', man, and I like the way he represents the running backs." Chargers coach Marty Schottenheimer had an even simpler take on the humble halfback. "He is the finest running back to ever wear an NFL uniform," he said.

Injuries and a tough schedule held the Chargers in check in 2005, and they finished third in their division with a 9–7 record. Yet another star emerged that season, as rookie linebacker Shawne Merriman delivered plenty of crushing tackles, recorded 10 sacks, and won NFL Rookie of the Year honors. After the season, the Chargers released Brees, officially handing the reins to the younger Rivers.

Merriman notched 17 sacks in 2006, although he missed four games due to a suspension for violating the NFL's steroid policy. With Rivers under center and another great season by Tomlinson, the team finished with a franchise-best 14–2 record. In the playoffs, the Chargers jumped out to a 14–10 first-half lead over the powerful New England

X Philip Rivers played brilliantly in his first season as a starter, slinging 22 touchdown passes and only 9 interceptions in 2006.

After his first three highlight-filled NFL seasons, intense linebacker Shawne Merriman missed all of 2008 with a knee injury.

Patriots. With 8 minutes and 35 seconds to go in the fourth

quarter, San Diego still held a 21–13 lead. An interception

by Chargers defensive back Marlon McCree appeared likely

to seal a San Diego victory, but the ball was stripped away

and recovered by the Patriots. New England then seized the

momentum, tying the game and then taking the lead. The

Chargers missed a 54-yard field goal, sending them to a

24–21 defeat—one of the most devastating playoff losses in

team history.

Frustrated by the playoff near misses, San Diego made

the controversial decision to fire Coach Schottenheimer in

the off-season and hired veteran coach Norv Turner in his

place. The team struggled early in 2007, but the midseason

pickup of wide receiver Chris Chambers and the emergence

of third-year receiver Vincent Jackson gave the San Diego

X A former standout with the Miami Dolphins, Chris Chambers made San Diego's offense even stronger with his mid-season arrival in 2007.

X Norv Turner came to San Diego with leadership experience in both the NFC and AFC, having previously coached the Washington Redskins and Oakland Raiders.

offense a boost. The Chargers finished with an 11–5 record, tops in the AFC West once again. After defeating the Tennessee Titans and Indianapolis Colts, the Chargers had a chance to take revenge on the Patriots in the AFC Championship Game. Once again, though, the Patriots were too powerful, sending the Chargers home by a score of 21–12.

That loss seemed to take the wind out of San Diego's sails in 2008. While players such as Rivers, Gates, and cornerback Antonio Cromartie gave some fine performances, Tomlinson appeared to have finally lost a step, and the club dropped several painfully close games as it started 4–8. Refusing to quit, though, the Chargers won their last four games to recapture their division, then won a playoff game over the Colts before their season finally ended.

SAN DIEGO DISCO

Many sports teams have a fight song. Usually they are short, simple, and designed to pump up the crowd. They are not usually disco! During the mid-1970s, Chargers owner Gene Klein watched his team struggle on the field and at the ticket office. By 1980, Klein decided that drastic measures were necessary to put some life into his struggling franchise. He launched a multimedia campaign, complete with a new slogan, T-shirts, decals, and a new Chargers theme song, "San Diego Super Chargers." As the team gained success on the field, the disco-flavored song kept fans singing in the stands every time the Chargers put points on the board. Nearly three decades later, the song, recorded by Captain Q.B. and the Big Boys, remains as popular as ever—except with opposing teams. "I hate that song," said New England Patriots head coach Bill Belichick. "It means it's not going well for us." Chargers fans, however, loved belting out such lyrics as, "With high voltage play, we won't let up a minute, we're going all the way—all the way!"

ON THE **SIDELINES**

SAN DIEGO GETS TOO HOT

Every now and then, events transpire that remind professional sports teams that the game they play is just a game. Twice in the last decade, the San Diego Chargers faced such an event. In 2003, wildfires burned more than 700,000 acres in Southern California, causing residents to flee their homes in search of safety. Qualcomm Stadium, the Chargers' home, became a sanctuary for many. The Chargers had to move a Monday Night Football game against the Miami Dolphins to Arizona State's Sun Devil Stadium while Qualcomm was used as a shelter for fire refugees. Sadly, the scene was repeated on an even larger scale in the fall of 2007. Fires again blazed through Southern California, and more than 900,000 people were displaced. Thousands moved into the stadium and found more than they expected, as their neighbors did their best to make them comfortable with emergency supplies. After the 2003 fires, former Chargers linebacker Junior Seau put the situation in perspective, saying, "The game of football is secondary right now, and I hate to see it happen to my hometown or any hometown."

From the glory days of the early 1960s to the Air Coryell era to the Super Bowl season of 1994, the team with the lightning bolt logo has earned its share of AFL and NFL success over the past four decades. And with an all-time roster that features such names as Alworth, Hadl, Fouts, and Tomlinson, San Diego has been represented by some of the greatest players ever to wear cleats. As today's Chargers continue to fight toward a Super Bowl championship, their fans can't wait for lightning to strike.

X A cornerback with blistering speed, Antonio Cromartie (number 31) helped the Chargers make playoff runs in 2006, 2007, and 2008.

INDEX